Here's all the great literature in this grade level of *Celebrate Reading!*

EAT UP, GEMMA

Written by
Sarah Hayes

Illustrated by
Jan Ormerod

The Doorbell Rang
by Pat Hutchins

When the
Elephant
Walks

Keiko Kasza

Finding a Starting Point

Big Books & Little Books

It's a Perfect Day!
by Abigail Pizer
✹ CHILDREN'S CHOICE AUTHOR

Peanut Butter and Jelly
Illustrations by
Nadine Bernard Westcott
✹ CHILDREN'S CHOICE ILLUSTRATOR

The Gunnywolf
retold and illustrated
by A. Delaney
✹ CHILDREN'S CHOICE

So Can I
by Allan Ahlberg
✹ CHILDREN'S BOOK AWARD AUTHOR

One Gorilla
by Atsuko Morozumi
✹ *NEW YORK TIMES* BEST ILLUSTRATED

Mary Had a Little Lamb
by Sarah Josepha Hale
Photographs by
Bruce McMillan
✹ ALA NOTABLE ILLUSTRATOR

Featured Poet

David McCord

BOOK B

Hurry, Furry Feet

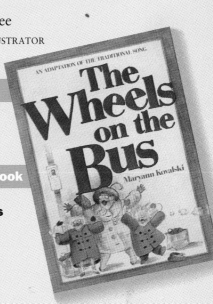

Old Hat, New Hat
by Stan and Jan Berenstain
✳ MICHIGAN YOUNG READER
AWARD AUTHORS

The Foot Book and
Hurry, Hurry, Hurry
by Dr. Seuss
✳ CALDECOTT HONOR ILLUSTRATOR
✳ LAURA INGALLS WILDER AWARD
AUTHOR/ILLUSTRATOR

My Street Begins at My House
by Ella Jenkins
Illustrations by
James E. Ransome
✳ PARENTS' CHOICE SONGWRITER

When the Elephant Walks
by Keiko Kasza
✳ ALA NOTABLE AUTHOR

Sitting in My Box
by Dee Lillegard
Illustrations by Jon Agee
✳ NEW YORK TIMES BEST ILLUSTRATOR

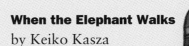
Featured Poet

Evelyn Beyer

Big Book & Little Book

The Wheels on the Bus
by Maryann Kovalski

BOOK C

Our Singing Planet

Featured Poets

N. M. Bodecker
Rowena Bennett
Mary Ann Hoberman
Lee Bennett Hopkins

Big Book & Little Book

BOOK D

My Favorite Foodles

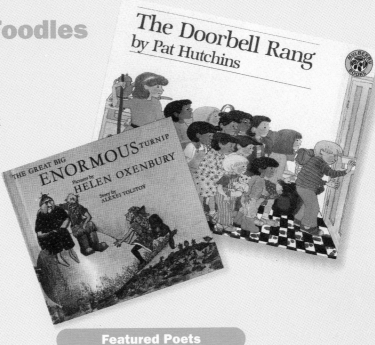

Featured Poets

Eve Merriam
Lucia and James L. Hymes, Jr.
Dennis Lee
John Ciardi
Charlotte Zolotow

Big Book & Little Book

BOOK E
Happy Faces

Featured Poets

Eloise Greenfield
Karla Kuskin
Myra Cohn Livingston

Big Book & Little Book

BOOK F
A Canary with Hiccups

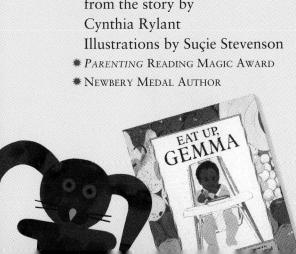

Celebrate Reading!
Big Book Bonus

My Favorite Foodles

Titles in This Set

About the Cover Artist
Steven Mach lives in downtown Chicago, where he draws,
paints, whistles and runs by the lake. His work enlivens
greeting cards, giftbags, books, and an occasional map
of Guam.

ISBN 0-673-82084-X

1995 Printing
Copyright © 1993
Scott, Foresman and Company, Glenview, Illinois
All Rights Reserved.
Printed in the United States of America.

Acknowledgments appear on page 128.

12345678910 VHJ 999897969594

My Favorite Foodles

ScottForesman

A Division of HarperCollins*Publishers*

Contents

Something Tasty

Give It a Try

6

Is Anybody Home?

Something Tasty

8

The Doorbell Rang

by Pat Hutchins

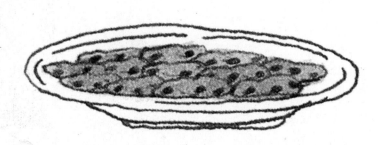

"I've made some cookies for tea,"
said Ma.

"Good," said Victoria and Sam.
"We're starving."

"Share them between yourselves,"
said Ma. "I made plenty."

"That's six each," said Sam and Victoria.
"They look as good as Grandma's," said Victoria.
"They smell as good as Grandma's," said Sam.

"No one makes cookies like Grandma,"
said Ma as the doorbell rang.

It was Tom and Hannah from next door.
"Come in," said Ma.
"You can share the cookies."

"That's three each," said Sam and Victoria.
"They smell as good as your Grandma's,"
 said Tom.
"And look as good," said Hannah.

"No one makes cookies like Grandma,"
said Ma as the doorbell rang.

It was Peter and his little brother.
"Come in," said Ma.
"You can share the cookies."

"That's two each," said Victoria and Sam.
"They look as good as your Grandma's,"
 said Peter. "And smell as good."

"Nobody makes cookies like Grandma,"
    said Ma as the doorbell rang.

It was Joy and Simon
with their four cousins.

"Come in," said Ma.
"You can share the cookies."

"That's one each," said Sam and Victoria.
"They smell as good as your Grandma's," said Joy.
"And look as good," said Simon.

"No one makes cookies like Grandma,"
said Ma as the doorbell rang

and rang.

"Oh dear," said Ma as the children stared
at the cookies on their plates.

"Perhaps you'd better eat them before
 we open the door."
"We'll wait," said Sam.

It was Grandma with an enormous
tray of cookies.

"How nice to have so many friends
  to share them with," said Grandma.
"It's a good thing I made a lot!"

"And no one makes cookies like Grandma,"
said Ma as the doorbell rang.

The Day My Doorbell Rang

by Pat Hutchins

I once invited eight people to come for lunch. I didn't know how many more friends my husband had invited.

On the day of the lunch, the doorbell kept ringing and ringing. Thirty people came to eat!

I decided to use the idea when I wrote The Doorbell Rang.

Pat Hutchins

AIKEN DRUM

There was a man lived in the moon, in the moon,
    in the moon.
There was a man lived in the moon and his
    name was Aiken Drum.

And he played upon a ladle, a ladle, a ladle.
He played upon a ladle and his
    name was Aiken Drum.

And his hat was made of good cream cheese,
good cream cheese, good cream cheese.
His hat was made of good cream cheese and his
name was Aiken Drum.

And his coat was made of good roast beef,
good roast beef, good roast beef.
His coat was made of good roast beef and his
name was Aiken Drum.

And his buttons were made of purple grapes,
purple grapes, purple grapes.
His buttons were made of purple grapes and his
name was Aiken Drum.

And his pants were made of celery stalks,
celery stalks, celery stalks.
His pants were made of celery stalks and his
name was Aiken Drum.

And he played upon a ladle, a ladle, a ladle.
He played upon a ladle and his
name was Aiken Drum.

There was a man lived in the moon, in the moon,
   in the moon.
There was a man lived in the moon and his
   name was Aiken Drum.

LUNCH BOX

by Eve Merriam

Lunch box, lunch box,
what's for lunch?
Peanut butter sandwich
and celery to crunch,
carrots and banana
and an apple to munch.
A bite and a bite
and a *bite* and a BITE,
now I'm heavy
and my lunch box is light.

Oudles of Noodles

by Lucia and James L. Hymes, Jr.

I love noodles. Give me oodles.
Make a mound up to the sun.
Noodles are my favorite foodles.
I eat noodles by the ton.

Anna Banana

by Dennis Lee

Anna Banana, jump into the stew:
Gravy and carrots are *good* for you.
Good for your teeth, and your fingernails too.
So, Anna Banana, jump into the stew!

Give It a Try

THE GREAT, BIG, ENORMOUS TURNIP

Retold by Alexei Tolstoy

Illustrations by Helen Oxenbury

Once upon a time, an old man planted a little turnip and said,
"Grow, grow, little turnip, grow sweet. Grow, grow, little turnip, grow strong."

49

And the turnip grew up sweet and strong,
and big and enormous.
Then, one day, the old man went to pull it up.
He pulled and pulled again, but he could not
pull it up.

He called the old woman.

The old woman pulled the old man.
The old man pulled the turnip.
And they pulled and pulled again, but they
could not pull it up.

So the old woman called her granddaughter.

The granddaughter pulled the old woman.
The old woman pulled the old man.
The old man pulled the turnip.
And they pulled and pulled again, but they could not pull it up.

The granddaughter called the black dog.

61

The black dog pulled the granddaughter.
The granddaughter pulled the old woman.
The old woman pulled the old man.
The old man pulled the turnip.
And they pulled and pulled again, but they
could not pull it up.

63

The black dog called the cat.

65

The cat pulled the dog.
The dog pulled the granddaughter.
The granddaughter pulled the old woman.
The old woman pulled the old man.
The old man pulled the turnip.
And they pulled and pulled again,
but still they could not pull it up.

The cat called the mouse.

The mouse pulled the cat.
The cat pulled the dog.
The dog pulled the granddaughter.
The granddaughter pulled the old woman.
The old woman pulled the old man.
The old man pulled the turnip.

They pulled and pulled again,
and up came the turnip at last.

73

74

Wouldn't You?

by John Ciardi

If I
Could go
As high
And low
As the wind
As the wind
As the wind
Can blow—

I'd go!

From Seeds to Zucchinis

by Lulu Delacre

Winter is over.
The sun warms the earth.
My friends and I get rakes,
good soil, a packet of seeds,
and a water hose.

It's time to start our garden.
It's time to plant zucchini seeds.

Pat reads that we should first
loosen the soil.

Marcos and I rake and rake.

When we finish raking,
I can't wait to plant the seeds!

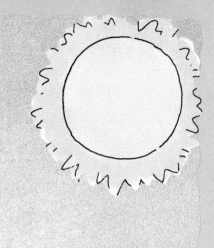

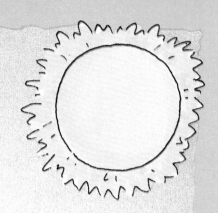

Marcos opens the packet
of seeds.

Pat tells us that next we have
to plant the seeds in rows
three feet apart.

Then we spread a thin layer
of soil over the seeds.

Finally, it's time to water
and wait.

Pat comes every day to look
at the garden.

He waters the seeds
unless it rains.

One day, Pat calls us to look at
the sprouts.
So many sprouts!

Some sprouts are little, and some
are big and strong.
Marcos pulls out the little ones
so the other sprouts have
room to grow.

With sun and water every day,
the zucchini plants grow,
and grow,
and grow
until they have big wide leaves
and bright, yellow flowers.

Then, thin zucchinis grow
under many flowers.

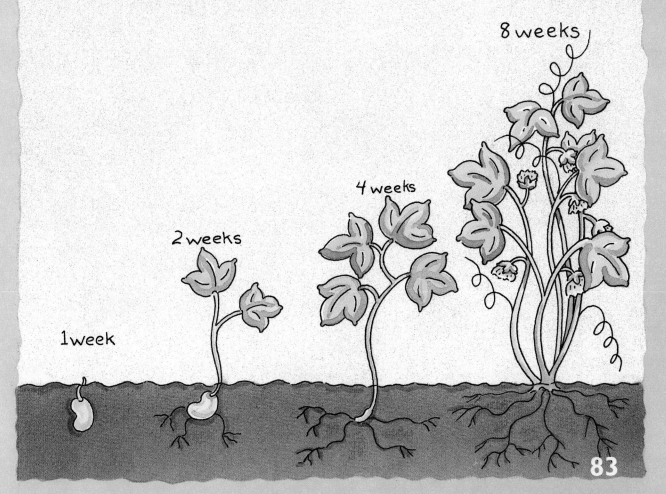

The flowers fall.

Surprise! The zucchinis are
much larger now
and are ready to pick.

We've done it!
Together we've grown
zucchinis from seeds.

Lulu Writes to You

Have you ever seen a real zucchini? I have. My daughters and I decided to plant zucchini seeds in our garden.

What surprises we had when we saw how the seeds turned into zucchinis!

With our first harvest, we baked two loaves of honey-zucchini bread. They were gone in two days!

That's why I decided to write about growing zucchinis.

Lulu Delacre

Is Anybody Home?

87

HELLO, HOUSE!

Retold by Linda Hayward   Illustrations by Lynn Munsinger

Brer Wolf is
full of ways
to get
Brer Rabbit.

Brer Rabbit is
full of ways to
trick Brer Wolf.

Brer Wolf
is bigger.

But
Brer Rabbit
is a whole
lot smarter.

One day Brer Rabbit
and Mrs. Rabbit
and the little Rabs
go on a picnic.

Brer Wolf hides

in their house.

He will catch

Brer Rabbit this time.

By and by

Brer Rabbit

comes back.

He feels funny.

Why is the door open?

94

Brer Rabbit peeks
in the window.
But he doesn't
see anything.

Brer Rabbit listens
at the chimney.
But he doesn't
hear anything.

Brer Rabbit steps up

to the door.

Does he go inside?

No!

Brer Rabbit has

more sense

than that!

Instead

he begins

to holler.

"HELLO, HOUSE!"

Brer Wolf is surprised.

Can houses talk?

Brer Wolf waits.

Brer Wolf listens.

But the house doesn't
say anything.

"Something is wrong!"

shouts Brer Rabbit.

"The house doesn't say

'HELLO TO YOU TOO!'"

"HELLO TO YOU TOO!"
calls Brer Wolf
in a low voice.

Brer Rabbit chuckles.

Now he knows something.

He knows Brer Wolf

is in his house!

"That house
talks too low,"
shouts Brer Rabbit.

"HELLO TO YOU TOO!"

calls Brer Wolf

in a high voice.

"That house
talks too high,"
shouts Brer Rabbit.

"HELLO TO YOU TOO!"
calls Brer Wolf
in a voice
not too high
and not too low.

109

"Brer Wolf!"
says Brer Rabbit.
"You can try and try.
But you will never
sound like a house."

Brer Wolf is mad!

Now he knows something.

He knows Brer Rabbit

has tricked him again!

Brer Wolf comes out.

He runs off.

He is glad

to get away

from Brer Rabbit

and his tricks.

Brer Rabbit

and his family

go inside.

"Hello, house!"

says Brer Rabbit.

But the house

doesn't say anything.

Houses don't talk,

you know!

DEAR CHILDREN,

What do you like to draw? I enjoyed working on Hello, House! because animals are my favorite things to draw.

The first thing I did when I began work was to go to the library and look at photographs of real rabbits. I brought my sketchbook and drew lots of different rabbits.

Then I did the same for the wolf.

Once I used my dog Winnie as a model for a character in a book. The only problem was that she was not very good at holding still!

Lynn Munsinger

Lynn Munsinger

A House

by Charlotte Zolotow

Everyone has a house,
  a house,
everyone has a house.
The bear has a cave,
the bird a nest,
the mole a hole,
but what is best
is a house like ours
    with windows and doors
    and rugs and floors.

Everyone has a house,
  a house,
everyone has a house.

119

Books to Enjoy

Wednesday Is Spaghetti Day
by Maryann Cocca-Leffler

Do you think pets just sleep when they are left home alone? Take a peek, and be ready for a tasty surprise!

Little Bear
by Else Holmelund Minarik
Illustrations by Maurice Sendak

Little Bear plans to fly as high as the moon. Is he ready to go?

The Wolf's Chicken Stew
by Keiko Kasza

A wolf wants to trick a hen and her chicks. Will his trick work?

Jasper's Beanstalk
by Nick Butterworth and Mick Inkpen

This story begins on Monday when Jasper finds a bean. What do you think happens many days later after he mows his bean plant?

Building a House
by Byron Barton

A family wants a house built on a green hill. Many people, tools, and machines have to get busy.

Goldilocks and the Three Bears
by James Marshall

A girl uses a bear family's house and food. Oh, oh—here come the bears!

Glossary

Words from your stories

Bb

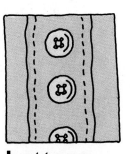

buttons

button

A **button** is used to hold clothes together. Some shirts have **buttons** down the front. **buttons**

Cc

catch

catch

Catch means to take and hold something moving. **caught, catching**

cookie

A **cookie** is a small, flat cake. **cookies**

Dd

doesn't

Doesn't means does not.

Gg

grandma

Grandma means grandmother. **grandmas**

grandma

grow

Grow means to get bigger. Children **grow** every year. **grew, grown, growing**

Hh

hide

Hide means to try to keep out of sight. My kitten always **hides** from the big dog. **hid, hidden, hiding**

hide

Ii

inside

John stayed **inside** because it was raining.

Ll

ladle

ladle

A **ladle** is a large, cup-shaped spoon with a long handle. Use a **ladle** to put soup in this bowl. **ladles**

Mm

moon

moon

The **moon** is the biggest and brightest thing in the sky at night. The **moon** goes around the Earth.

Oo

open

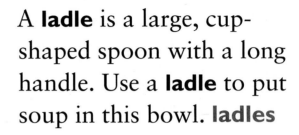

open

When you **open** something, people and things can get in or out. **opened, opening**

Pp

plenty

Plenty means enough. There is plenty of food for everyone.

pull

Pull means to move something toward you. It is hard to **pull** weeds from the ground. **pulled, pulling**

pull

Rr

rake

A **rake** is a kind of tool. **Rakes** are used in yards or gardens. **rakes**

rake

Ss

share

When you **share,** you let someone have a part of something. **shared, sharing**

share

smell

smell

A **smell** is something that you breathe in. The freshly baked bread **smelled** good. **smelled, smelling**

Tt

trick

A **trick** is something done to make people laugh or to fool them. She **tricked** me by hiding behind the door. **tricked, tricking**

turnip

turnip

A **turnip** is a round, white or yellow vegetable that grows underground. **turnips**

126

Vv

voice

Your **voice** is the sound you make with your mouth. You use your **voice** to talk and sing. **voices**

Ww

wait

Wait means to stay where you are. People **wait** for something to happen or for someone to come. **waited, waiting**

Zz

zucchini

A **zucchini** is a long, dark-green vegetable. **Zucchinis** grow on top of the ground. **zucchinis**

zucchini

Acknowledgments

Text

Page 10: *The Doorbell Rang* by Pat Hutchins. Copyright © 1986 by Pat Hutchins. Published by Greenwillow Books, a Division of William Morrow & Company, Inc. Reprinted by permission of William Morrow and Company, Inc.

Page 33: "The Day My Doorbell Rang" by Pat Hutchins. Copyright © 1991 by Pat Hutchins.

Page 34: "Aiken Drum" from the book *The Fireside Book of Children's Songs* collected and edited by Marie Winn. Copyright © 1966. Used by permission of the publisher, Simon and Schuster, New York, NY.

Page 42: "Lunch Box" from *You Be Good and I'll Be Night* by Eve Merriam. Text copyright © 1988 by Eve Merriam. Published by Morrow Junior Books. Reprinted by permission of William Morrow and Company, Inc.

Page 44: "Oodles of Noodles" from *Oodles of Noodles and Other Hymes' Rhymes* by Lucia and James L. Hymes, Jr. Copyright © 1964 by Addison-Wesley Publishing Company, Inc. Reprinted with permission of the publisher.

Page 45: "Anna Banana" by Dennis Lee. Reprinted by permission of MGA Agency.

Page 48: Illustrations copyright © Helen Oxenbury 1968 from *The Great, Big, Enormous Turnip* by permission of Heinemann Young Books.

Page 76: "Wouldn't You?" by John Ciardi. From *You Read to Me, I'll Read to You.* Harper & Row, copyright © 1962 by John Ciardi. Reprinted by permission of the estate of John Ciardi.

Page 78: *From Seeds to Zucchinis* by Lulu Delacre. Copyright © 1991 by Lulu Delacre.

Page 85: "Lulu Writes to You" by Lulu Delacre. Copyright © 1991 by Lulu Delacre.

Page 88: *Hello, House!* by Linda Hayward, illustrated by Lynn Munsinger. Text copyright © 1988 by Random House, Inc. Illustrations copyright © 1988 by Lynn Munsinger. Reprinted by permission of Random House, Inc.

Page 116: "Dear Children," by Lynn Munsinger. Copyright © 1991 by Lynn Munsinger.

Page 118: "A House" by Charlotte Zolotow. Reprinted by permission of the author.

Artists

Illustrations owned and copyrighted by the illustrator.
Seymour Chwast, 4–9, 46–47, 86–87, 120–127
Pat Hutchins, 10–32
Richard McNeel, 34–41
Steven Mach, 44
Elizabeth Allen, 45
Helen Oxenbury, 48–75
Linda Kelen, 76–77
Leslie Wolf, 78–85
Lynn Munsinger, 88–117
Pamela Rossi, 118–119

Photographs

Page 33: Courtesy of Pat Hutchins.
Page 85: Courtesy of Lulu Delacre.
Page 117: Alan Shortall (Courtesy of Lynn Munsinger.)

Glossary

The contents of the Glossary have been adapted from *My First Picture Dictionary,* copyright © 1990 Scott, Foresman and Company; *My Second Picture Dictionary,* copyright © 1990 Scott, Foresman and Company; and *Beginning Dictionary,* copyright © 1993 Scott, Foresman and Company.